SCS

e 2

e 14

D1494589

**Stories
illustrated by
Martin Chatterton
and
Fitz Hammond**

In this story

 Ben

 Ruby

 Mum

Tricky words

- Clone-O-Mat
- copy
- clone
- machine
- another
- screamed
- sucked
- dial

Introduce these tricky words and help the reader when they come across them later!

Story starter

Ben lives with his mum and dad and his sister, Ruby. Ben loves to invent new machines. One day, he made a Clone-O-Mat that could make a copy of someone if they went inside it.

Ben and the Clone Machine

Ben ran out of the shed.
"Look, Ruby, I have made a
Clone-O-Mat," he said.

"If you go into my Clone-O-Mat, it will make a copy of you," said Ben. "You could get your clone to do jobs for you."

"Your clone could tidy your room for you," said Ben.
"Your Clone-O-Mat will not work," said Ruby. "Your machines are rubbish!"

Ben went into the house.

Ruby looked at the Clone-O-Mat.

POP!

Ruby went into the Clone-O-Mat.

POP! The machine made

another Ruby.

"I am Ruby!" said the clone.

"No, *I* am Ruby!" said Ruby.

The machine went POP! again.

There was **ANOTHER** Ruby.

POP! POP! POP! The machine made lots of Ruby clones. Just then, Ben came out of the house.

He saw all the Ruby clones.

"Run, Ruby, run!" said Ben.

Ruby ran around the garden
but all the clones ran after her.
"Ben! Do something!"
screamed Ruby.

Ben turned a dial on the
Clone-O-Mat.
The clones were sucked back
into the machine.
But Ruby was still screaming!

Mum came out of the house.

"Ruby!" said Mum. "Stop screaming, or no pocket money!"

"My Clone-O-Mat works well!"
said Ben.

"Yes," said Ruby. "It works *too* well!"

Quiz

- What happened when Ruby used the Clone-O-Mat?
- Why did Ruby say the machine worked 'too well'?
- Would you like to have a clone of yourself?

Word Detective

- Phonic Assessment: Long vowels
  Page 4: Sound out the four phonemes (sounds) in 'clone'. What long vowel sound can you hear?
- Page 4: Sound out the three phonemes (sounds) in 'make'. What long vowel sound can you hear?
- Page 6: Sound out the three phonemes (sounds) in 'made'. What long vowel sound can you hear?

Super Speller

Can you spell these words from memory?

have   went   there

HA! HA! HA!

Q What happens if you clone a witch?

A You won't be able to tell which witch is witch!

Before Reading

In this story

 Sam

 Sam's mum

 A great big spider

Tricky words

- packet
- shelf
- shrank
- stuck
- spider
- floor
- tasty
- idea

Introduce these tricky words and help the reader when they come across them later!

Story starter

Whenever Sam's mum asks Sam to do a *little* job, he shrinks! One day, Sam's mum asked him to get her a packet of seeds from the shed.

Shrinking Sam
and the
Spider

Sam was in the shed.

His mum called to him.

"Do a little job for me," she said.

"Get me that packet of seeds from the shelf."

There was a great big **FLASH** and Sam shrank!

This always happened when his mum asked him to do a *little* job.

Now Sam was tiny!

Sam grabbed the packet of seeds.

But he was stuck on the shelf.

How could he get down?

Suddenly, he saw a great big spider.
And the spider saw Sam.

"Mmm," said the spider. "You look very tasty!"

"No!" cried Sam. "Don't eat me!"
Then Sam saw the spider's web.
The web went right down to
the floor. Sam had an idea.

"Look down there!" said Sam. "There is a big tasty fly! I'll get on your back and take you to the fly."

"OK," said the spider.

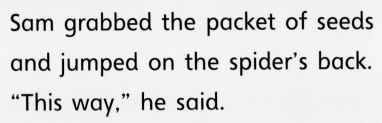

Sam grabbed the packet of seeds
and jumped on the spider's back.
"This way," he said.
And the spider ran down its web
to the floor.

SEEDS

"Now, where is this fly?"
said the spider.
"It's just there," said Sam.
The spider looked.

"That's not a big tasty fly," said the
spider. "It's just a leaf! You tricked
me. Now I'm going to eat you."

But Sam jumped off the spider's back and **FLASH** Sam was the right size again.

Just then, Sam's mum said, "Did you find those seeds?"

"Yes, Mum!" said Sam.

"But it was a tricky little job!"

Quiz

Text Detective

- Why did Sam have to go on the spider's back?
- Why did Sam say it was a 'tricky little job'?
- Was it fair of Sam to trick the spider?

Word Detective

- **Phonic Assessment:** Long vowels
  Page 19: Sound out the three phonemes (sounds) in 'right'.
  What long vowel sound can you hear?
- Page 20: Sound out the three phonemes (sounds) in 'take'.
  What long vowel sound can you hear?
- Page 23: Sound out the four phonemes (sounds) in 'seeds'.
  What long vowel sound can you hear?

Super Speller

Can you spell these words from memory?

take   from   down

HA! HA! HA!

Q Why didn't the spider feel well?

A It had caught a nasty bug.